blackbird & company
WRITING DISCOVERY GUIDE

Intro to Composition:

The Essay

VOLUME 1

Essay as Structure: Become an Architect

by Kimberly Bredberg, MFA
contributing editors, Sara Evans, Tracey Lane

Visit us at
blackbirdandcompany.com
and explore our full range of Discovery guides:

Earlybird Literature & Writing
GRADES K-2

Literature & Writing
GRADES 2-12

Intro to Composition
GRADES 5-12

Exploring Poetry
GRADES 5-12

Research Science
GRADES 5-9

Copyright © 2016 by Blackbird & Company Educational Press.

All rights reserved. No part of this book may be reproduced or utilized in any form or by any electronic or mechanical means, including photocopying, without permission in writing from the publisher except for the use of brief quotations in a book review.

Printed in the U.S.A.

First Printing, 2016

ISBN 978-1-937200-62-6

V1 01 Jan 2016

www.blackbirdandcompany.com

Table of Contents

INTRODUCTION 4

FOR THE TEACHER 6
   Pre-Writing Exercises 6
   Evaluation 7
   Writing Evaluation Rubric 8

FOR THE STUDENT 9
   Before You Begin 9
   The Writing Process 10
   The Architecture of Good Writing 11
   Developing Your Voice 12
   The Writer's Toolkit 13
   More About Active and Passive Voice 14
   The Structure of an Essay 16

ESSAY AS STRUCTURE: BECOME AN ARCHITECT! 17
   Lesson 1 (week 1): Getting Started, part 1 18
   Lesson 1 (week 2): Getting Started, part 1 (cont.) 22
   Lesson 2 (week 3): The Introduction, part 1 26
   Lesson 2 (week 4): The Introduction, part 1 (cont.) 29
   Lesson 3 (week 5): The Introduction, part 2 33
   Lesson 3 (week 6): The Introduction, part 2 (cont.) 36
   Lesson 4 (week 7): The Body 40
   Lesson 4 (week 8): The Body (cont.) 43
   Lesson 5 (week 9): The Conclusion 47
   Lesson 5 (week 10): The Conclusion (cont.) 51

NOTES 57

> Fill your paper
> with the breathings
> of your heart.
>
> – William Wordsworth

Great Essays

Just as no two fingerprints are alike, every author has a distinct writing style. Voice is the fingerprint of an author. Architectural structures are embellished with the voice of the architect. Essays are embellished with the voice of the writer. Blackbird & Company Writing Discovery Guides have been developed with the fundamental belief that great writing begins with great ideas. As young writers develop confidence in their ability to express their ideas, they will recognize and embrace the power of writing.

The purpose of writing is to communicate.

Students will actively engage in the work of transforming a cluster of abstract thoughts into a single big idea. This course teaches them to coherently communicate that idea within a focused structure while drawing the reader into their thoughts. *Activities will emphasize content, process, strategy, mechanical conventions, and style.*

Writing is for a reader.

Everything that is read, was once written by someone who had an idea. An essay can have many purposes, but ultimately it must first engage the reader. Unless the essay engages the reader, its underlying purposes—to instruct, to convince, to convey—will be lost. *Writing directives will guide the writer through the process of crafting words and develop their awareness of audience and purpose.*

Big ideas can be communicated through a range of writing domains, including creative writing. It is vital that students discover and explore the potential of all types. Some writing describes, some narrates, some exposes, and some persuades. Some writing is simply meant to entertain. All writing has the power to inform. *This 10 week course will focus on composing the descriptive and literary essay.*

Great essays have the power to encourage, empower, and enlighten. For this reason essay writing should not just be treated as a mechanical endeavor, but as a pathway for the writer to communicate the depths of the heart and mind.

Take flight!

For the Teacher

TEACH STUDENTS TO WRITE FOR REAL:
Before embarking on any writing adventure with your students, remember to keep at the forefront of your mind that becoming a writer is a lifelong process.

Too often, the student writer's idea is squelched by the daunting task of getting the grammar and mechanics to toe the line. When students are encouraged to value the work of developing an original idea, form follows function and the writer's idea is elevated. Great essays have the power to encourage, empower, and enlighten. For this reason essay writing should not just be treated as a mechanical endeavor, but as a pathway for the writer to communicate the depths of the heart and mind.

So, the question should never be, "How do I teach my students to write?" But, rather, "How can I keep my students inspired to become authentic writers?"

FOLLOWING ARE TIPS TO HELP YOUR STUDENTS DEVELOP A TRADITION OF WRITING ALONG WITH GUIDELINES FOR EVALUATING THEIR WORK.

PRE-WRITING EXERCISES
Pre-writing is the most creative part of the writing process because this is where ideas are born. Often this first step—the *brainstorming* session—is precisely where writers get stuck.

Each week students will ponder and respond to a series of prompts that will challenge them to move ideas from the recesses of their mind to the paper in front of them. They will also explore vocabulary related to the topic at hand to lead them to a deeper understanding of the process. As writers move through these exercises, encourage them to note as many specific details as possible. This will enable them to develop stronger support for their big idea.

Young writers will want to RUSH this step (or skip it altogether!). However, this unit has been designed to guide students through a deliberate pre-writing process that will help them discover the slower, methodical pace that leads to thoughtful and powerful essays. It is a good idea to have your student read all content and prompts aloud to you for the first few weeks to make sure they are understanding the concepts, and how the unit flows and functions.

READ, READ, READ!
Books are great mentors and reading them has a profound effect on a writer's development. Explore the way writers craft language and develop their voice. Lead students on a journey through passages from great stories and you will empower them to discover the wonder of words.

MINE FOR WORDS AND PHRASES
What do you notice about vocabulary? Can a single word make a significant impact? How do writers shape words into phrases? Can a small phrase make a significant impact? How do words and phrases affect the rhythm of writing? How do words and phrases impact what the reader senses? When students connect to language they become confident, imaginative writers who produce coherent and creative essays that are communicated with a distinct voice.

START A WORD COLLECTION
Use a notebook or journal to start a word collection. Words can be found anywhere and everywhere! Challenge students to always be on the lookout for interesting or unknown words and of course, have them look up meanings for ones they don't know. Sometimes a single word can spark a whole idea!

READY, SET... WRITE!
Where do ideas come from? Nothing sparks student pencils more than a timer and a charge, "You have ten minutes to free write...GO!" Slamming ideas onto the page often produces little gems that can later be developed and shaped into a meaningful piece of writing. Encourage your students at the end of ten minutes to read what they wrote and to highlight ideas, concepts, phrases, words, anything that stands out to them as intriguing. Encourage them to bundle what they find in an idea book to develop later.

For the Teacher (cont.)

HAND STUDENTS A RED PEN

Rough drafts should only be written with a pencil or blue/black pen. Empower your students to then work through the self-editing process with a red pen before conferencing. Using a strong accent color will make the process from rough draft to final draft easier. You may also want to use a second accent color for any conferencing edits so it is clear who made what changes at what stage.

THE CONFERENCE, TIPS FOR THE EDITOR

Before conferencing with the editor (teacher), the writer (student) should first make self-edits to their rough draft, sweeping the writing for the usual checks—spelling, grammar, and punctuation—while also paying attention to readability, clarity, and creativity. At the end of each assignment there is a Student Self-Evaluation form to help with this process.

As an editor, the cardinal rule is to first read the student work as a reader, paying close attention to the flow of content. Ask yourself if the writing is engaging, is it communicating something believable? Do you enjoy what you are reading? Next, read it again as an editor. Ask yourself if the work is working mechanically. Are there bumpy spots where the writing takes you out as a reader? Do you get stuck on choppy sentence fragments? Are you left breathless by endless run-ons? Are there punctuation problems? Do you find the organization of the sub-topics stray?

After these two thorough readings, share your thoughts with the student who will go back into the writing to refine the structure, add flourishes, and incorporate details that will communicate the big idea more coherently and fluidly while maintaining vocal authenticity.

Once the writing is working on a communication level, the editor should do a thorough sweep for mechanical errors such as subject/verb agreement, punctuation, capitalization, spelling, sentence structure, and so on.

EVALUATING STUDENT WRITING

Always keep in mind:

Anyone can teach writing.

Anyone can evaluate writing.

First and foremost, you have to be a reader.

The writer is an architect. Ultimately, the purpose of any
writing is to shelter the writer's big idea. And so, the primary work of the editor is to read the essay (multiple times) and then ask:

→ Is the writer communicating the main idea and is it clearly defined?

→ Is the vocabulary powerful and engaging, does it spark striking imagery?

→ Are the details the writer uses to develop the big idea specific and meaningful?

→ Are the sentences well constructed, are they appropriately complex, or are you stumbling on fragments and run-ons?

→ Do the sentences vary in length to create an interesting rhythm?

→ Is the capitalization and punctuation correct?

→ Do the sentences flow into passages according to the blueprint of the essay for the single purpose of sheltering the writer's idea?

Once conferencing is complete, the student should type their final draft, incorporating all edits for clean, polished, ready-to-be-published work!

FOR FURTHER STUDY

In Lessons 1-5 of this unit students complete exercises in an outside workbook, *Thinking in Threes*. These exercises reinforce topics being presented and offer practice for each stage of the essay writing process. However, there are a few lessons that are not specifically assigned that students may complete to strengthen their writing skills.

» Extras, pages 85-95
  - Timed Writing
  - Planning Strategies
  - Suggested Topics
  - Sample Essays

Writing Evaluation Rubric

Use this rubric as a guideline when assessing your student's writing:

ACCOMPLISHED

- Creatively focuses on the topic
- Uses logical progression of ideas to develop and supports topic with details
- Varies sentence structure
- Uses interesting transitions
- Makes strong word choice
- Mature understanding of writing conventions

PROFICIENT

- Focuses on topic and includes adequate support
- Uses logical progression of ideas to develop and loosely supports topic
- Some varied sentence structure
- Transitions are adequate but not creative
- Word choice is adequate but not creative
- General understanding of writing conventions

BASIC

- Topic is addressed, but unclear
- Lacks logical progression of ideas and support is weak
- Sentences are stagnant and uninteresting
- Lack of transitions
- Average word choice
- Partial understanding of writing conventions

LIMITED

- Topic may be mentioned, but not clearly addressed and loosely supported
- Organization pattern is weak
- Writing contains sentence fragments and run-ons
- Poor transitions
- Poor word choice
- Definite misunderstanding of writing conventions

POOR

- Topic is not addressed or clearly supported
- Organizational pattern is lacking
- Sentence structure is insufficient
- Non-existent transitions
- Weak word choice
- Frequent errors in basic writing conventions

For the Student

It's true, an essay is a composition of words that communicate a specific idea in a distinct three part structure. But, an essay, most significantly, is your opportunity to weigh out and craft an original idea.

HOW THIS GUIDE IS ORGANIZED

This course is designed with you in mind and is intended to be self-directed, freeing you to authentically and creatively shape your original, big idea. This introduction to the structure and tools necessary to compose an essay includes exercises for strengthening your compositional skills and developing your voice. Each section of this course contains important information about mechanics, content, and voice that needs to be read and studied carefully. Resist the urge to skim! A thorough understanding of this material is crucial to successful essay writing.

CONTENTS:

For the Student:
- The Writing Process
- The Architecture of Good Writing
- Developing Your Voice
- The Writer's Toolkit
- More About Active/Passive Voice
- Structure of An Essay

Lessons:
- Lesson 1 (weeks. 1+2): Getting Started
- Lesson 2 (weeks 3+4): The Introduction
- Lesson 3 (weeks 5+6): The Introduction, cont.
- Lesson 4 (weeks 7+8): The Body
- Lesson 5 (weeks 9+10): The Conclusion

Each lesson is designed to be completed over the course of two weeks, spending 2-4 hours per week. During this time you will be exploring the structure and purpose of an essay, while gathering tools to strengthen your voice.

WHAT YOU WILL NEED

Have the following resources close at hand as you work through this guide:
- Dictionary
- Thesaurus
- *Thinking in Threes* workbook
- Red pen for editing

The Writing Process

Before they are ever built, architectural structures are first imagined. Materials are gathered and then, through a series of steps, from the foundation up, a structure is built. In writing, the *idea* is first imagined. Words are gathered to be crafted—words into phrases, phrases into sentences, sentences into passages—until at last, an idea is realized.

1. Imagine a big idea.

Brainstorming begins! Make a list, diagram, topic wheel, or outline to help organize your thoughts before you begin writing. **Remember, your ideas are important!**

2. Get your idea on paper.

It's called a rough draft for a reason! Don't worry about being perfect here. **Get your words out of your head and onto the page using a free flow of ideas.** Skip lines during this initial stage in the writing process so you can easily modify your ideas when you revise.

3. Conference, then revise your idea.

Before you get a second opinion, read your work aloud to yourself and then **ask someone else to read it.** See if the content conveys the idea you set out to communicate in a clear and stylish manner. Make sure your voice shines!

4. Proofread your idea.

Now that you've received feedback and made changes, **re-read your writing carefully**, making additional spelling, grammar, and punctuation edits where necessary.

5. Publish your idea.

Remember, your idea is a gift meant to be shared. Type out your polished final draft and share it with someone.

The Architecture of Good Writing

Mechanics is *Structure*

The **mechanics** of writing—punctuation, spelling, and grammar—are the tools you will use to shape words into sentences, to craft rhythm, and to inject meaning that will direct the reader through your written work. **Structure frames your big idea.**

Content is *Function*

The **content** of a written work is your big idea. Content might instruct, convince, convey, or entertain, but fundamentally, you must craft the content to capture the attention of the reader. **Content communicates your big idea.**

Voice is *Beauty*

The voice is the individuality of your writing. Language is shaped by the choices you make. No matter what you're writing about your single purpose is to captivate the imagination of the reader. **Voice is the one-of-a-kind fingerprint of the writer.**

Developing Your Voice

Crafting words involves a series of choices.

When it comes to writing, words are the raw materials. As you construct an essay, or for that matter any type of writing, consider meaning and sound. Use words that are familiar and become familiar with words that are unfamiliar. Building words into phrases and then into sentences is a complex task that is essential to communicating a specific idea and vital to injecting voice into an essay.

The best writing, the page-turning kind, is great because it is an authentic creation of an individual writer. Architectural structures are embellished with the voice of the architect. Essays are embellished with the voice of the writer.

The tricky thing is that each writer must do the work of grasping the potential of words, must understand how to shape those words and imagine all possible combinations of these components in order to develop and raise their voice.

In this unit, you are provided this very opportunity. Recognizing what tools are available and learning how to use them skillfully will add volume and flair to your voice.

> "The human voice is the organ of the soul."
>
> — Henry Wadsworth Longfellow

A writer should never be told when to use a tool, or how many tools to use, but rather, should have a well equipped toolkit readily available. When it comes to constructing words, phrases, sentences, and passages to shelter your big idea, the possibilities are endless.

The magnitude of language is immense—the toolkit provided on the next page will enable you to explore the potential of language.

The Writer's Toolkit

Imposition or *Preposition*

Prepositions are glorious little words! Use them to indicate a relationship between things and to add both detail and clarity to your writing. Prepositional phrases begin with a preposition and end with a noun. Sample prepositions: after, before, from, about, in, over, under, above, below.

The peaches <u>in the basket</u> are ready to be baked <u>into a pie</u>.

Not Santa, the Other *Clause*

Subordinate clauses bring a little something extra to a sentence by expanding your idea and adding specificity. A clause cannot stand alone because it is not a complete sentence. Clauses often begin with because, since, as, whenever, although, though, while, etc.

Liam ran for paper towels <u>as the spilled milk was dripping over the edge of the table</u>.

Positively *Appositive*

The **appositive** is an interjected phrase that gives more details about the next door noun. Remember to always punctuate your appositive phrase with commas.

Søren, <u>the youngest member of the family</u>, likes to crack jokes during dinner.

To Be or Not to Be, that is the *Infinitive*

An **infinitive** is simply a basic form of a verb and will almost always begin with "to." For example: to be, to sing, to love, to send, to sneeze

Sara was delighted <u>to see</u> her best friend after so many months away from her.

Zing-*ing*

Add "zing" and a sense of immediate action to sentences by opening with an "**ing**" word.

<u>Seeing</u> the race inspired Jack, who hoped to one day become a sprinter.

Ready, Set, *Active*

When writing in the **active voice** the subject is doing the action. Sentences are stronger, more direct, and very clear as to who is doing what.

My grandmother <u>mailed</u> me a care package on my birthday.

More About Active & Passive Voice

Writing in the passive voice is not always wrong. In fact, sometimes the passive voice is an effective stylistic technique. However, overuse of the verb "to be" can weaken the impression of a great idea. The passive voice has the inherent danger of ambiguity. Making an effort to understand how and when to use the active and passive voice in writing will help you build the habit of communicating in an interesting and clear manner.

In lessons 1-5, you will be developing this muscle by writing a single paragraph that speaks through one of the five human senses without incorporating any passive verbs.

Verbs have two "voices": ACTIVE *or* PASSIVE

When the subject of a sentence is doing the action, the verb voice is <u>ACTIVE</u>:

*Sandra **fed** the dog.*

When the subject of the sentence passively receives the action, the verb voice is <u>PASSIVE</u>:

*The dog **was fed** by Sandra.*

Active & Passive Voice (cont.)

For the exercises that follow, be sure to avoid using these passive "to be" verbs:

TENSE	SINGULAR	PLURAL
Present	I *am* you *are* he/she *is*	we *are* you *are* they *are*
Present perfect	I *have been* you *have been* he/she *has been*	we *have been* you *have been* they *have been*
Past	I *was* you *were* he/she *was*	we *were* you *were* they *were*
Past perfect	I *had been* you *had been* he/she *had been*	we *had been* you *had been* they *had been*
Future	I *will be* you *will be* he/she *will be*	we *will be* you *will be* they *will be*
Future perfect	I *will have been* you *will have been* he/she *will have been*	we *will have been* you *will have been* they *will have been*
Present progressive	I *am being* you *are being* he/she *is being*	we *are being* you *are being* they *are being*
Past progressive	I *was being* you *were being* he/she *was being*	we *were being* you *were being* they *were being*

The Structure of an Essay

INTRODUCTION

The first paragraph of an essay invites the reader into the writer's big idea. The essay begins with a general statement called the **hook** that *grabs the reader's attention*. The second sentence of your introduction provides **context** and sets the stage for your big idea. The introduction ends with a very important sentence called the **thesis statement** that clearly states the big idea and introduces the three sub-topics you will be using to support it.

BODY

The body of the essay consists of three paragraphs, structured according to a **blueprint**, which will fully develop the **three sub-topics** of the thesis statement and allow the reader to explore the architecture of the writer's big idea.

CONCLUSION

The last paragraph of the essay opens with a sentence that **weaves** the sub-topics together and leads the reader to the next sentence, an **echo** of the thesis statement. The essay ends with a thought provoking sentence called the **twist** that will leave the reader with a memorable snapshot of the writer's big idea.

Essay as Structure:
Become an Architect

Writers always begin by shaping a thesis statement that declares a big idea and gives the reader insight into the construction plan. At this point, the real work begins as the writer crafts the architectural details that will shelter that big idea. The purpose of this section is to gather the tools that will enable you to discover and delight in the process of shaping and crafting. These tools will help you communicate your big idea to an audience in the form of an essay.

- → Lesson 1 (weeks 1+2): Getting Started
- → Lesson 2 (weeks 3+4): The Introduction, part 1
- → Lesson 3 (weeks 5+6): The Introduction, part 2
- → Lesson 4 (weeks 7+8): The Body
- → Lesson 5 (weeks 9+10): The Conclusion

WEEK 1 – Getting Started

THE ESSAY – VOLUME 1 | **LESSON 1**

Lesson 1: Getting Started

Use a dictionary to define:

architecture

shelter (architectural definition)

structure (architectural definition)

Define in your own words:

essay

Now use a dictionary to define:

essay

WEEK 1 – Getting Started

One purpose of an architectural structure is to provide shelter.

Similarly, the essay consists of a distinct three-part structure that serves as a shelter for your idea.

Part 1: Introduction
The introduction is a very short presentation of your big idea in thesis form that hints at your plan to develop the idea in your body paragraphs. The thesis statement is your opportunity to lead the reader into the train of thought that will be developed throughout the essay.

Part 2: Body
The body consists of three paragraphs that develop your idea by exploring specific details and concepts in depth.

Part 3: Conclusion
The conclusion is a short paragraph that should echo your idea and leave your reader with something surprisingly meaningful to consider.

Good writing always begins with an idea you want to communicate to others. Just as architecture provides shelter, the foundational structure of an essay shelters your idea.

Think About It »
Architecture has many functions in addition to providing shelter. In some cases a square box might be all the structure you need, a place to find protection from the elements or a place to store your car. However, the next time you drive through a neighborhood, notice how each house becomes an individual home as the owner embellishes it with personal touches. Even though the structures are similar, there are distinct differences if you look closely.

Look around your city or town and observe different architectural structures. How are they similar? How are they unique? What shapes, colors, and materials do you notice? Look for examples and describe your findings.

WEEK 1 – Getting Started

THE ESSAY – VOLUME 1 | LESSON 1

> Now look again, in some cases a square box may be an adequate structural solution to a problem. A square box, however, is a completely inadequate structure for a grand monument or a place to house great works of art.
>
> *Architect Le Corbusier reminds us that, "Space and light and order. Those are the things that men need just as much as they need bread or a place to sleep."*

Think About It »

Architecture can do much more than meet our basic needs. Architecture can give us a sense of peace, a sense of wonder, it can be a canvas for creative expression, and it can communicate power and security.

The next time you drive around, notice the buildings that stand out from their surroundings. What is the basic function of the structure and how does it go beyond the basic function? What makes them stand out? Look for an example and describe your findings.

Workbook Assignments »

Complete the following assignments this week in *Thinking In Threes*.

❑ Pages 11-14: "The Power of Three"
❑ Pages 17-20: "Brainstorming"

WEEK 1 – Getting Started

BECOME AN ARCHITECT | LESSON 1

"Voice" Warm-Up »

This warm-up will help you practice different style techniques to develop your voice. Review pages 12—13 and then complete the following exercises.

Complete a sentence that begins with a preposition:

1. *After* the big storm, _____ .

Complete a sentence that begins with a clause:

2. *When the bell rang*, _____ .

Insert an appositive:

3. Hannah, _____ , earned her spot in the orchestra.

Complete a sentence that begins with an "ing" word:

4. *Singing* in the rain, _____ .

Complete a sentence that begins with an infinitive:

5. *To send* a text during the speaker's introduction _____ .

Change the sentences to active voice:

6. My neighbor's house *was painted* green last week.

7. Kristen *was tickled* by her brother every time she fell asleep on the couch.

Change the sentences to passive voice:

8. The surfer *wears* a wet suit when the water is especially cold.

9. *Leaving* dirty dishes in the sink discourages mother.

WEEK 2 – Getting Started

Lesson 1: Getting Started (cont.)

"Voice" Writing Exercise »

Write Through the Senses: SIGHT

As writers, we gather details that will spark the reader's senses. This week write a paragraph through the sense of sight, **avoiding all passive verbs**, incorporating instead strong, active verbs. Use as many of the voice techniques as possible. Remember, this is a voice exercise and, as such, may sound stilted. **The purpose is to experiment with language and gain confidence using the tools that will elevate your voice.**

Example of writing through the sense of *sight*:

> *Flashing red, green, orange, and blue billboards* **compete** for my attention as I **saunter** dazedly down *Times Square. Psychedelic lights* **replace** the *moon and stars* in the *Manhattan night sky*. Scores of *people* **walk** determinedly past me like an *army of robots outfitted in black winter coats. The New Yorkers do not* **cast** *a single glance at an overwhelmed tourist like myself. Shiny black skyscrapers* **tower** *above me from all sides. People* **shuffle** *in and out of stores* that cater to every sized pocket book. I **walk** past various electronic shops *simultaneously displaying cameras, stereos, and TV's at deceivingly low prices. Neon white light* **illuminates** the sidewalk in front of a Rolex Watch store. *The nightly news anchor* **looks** *down at me placidly from giant TV screens suspended in the night.* In the distance *King Kong* **clutches** *an enormous Empire State Building made entirely out of LEGOs.*

Begin your sight paragraph by brainstorming some topic ideas:

_____

_____

_____

Now, generate a list of descriptive sight words:

_____

_____

_____

Finally, compile a list of active verbs you might use for this paragraph:

_____

_____

_____

On the following two pages, write a rough draft and a final draft of your paragraph »

WEEK 2 – Getting Started

BECOME AN ARCHITECT | **LESSON 1**

SIGHT Paragraph » *Rough Draft*

Begin drafting your sight paragraph. Use a highlighter to find your verbs and make sure you have not used the passive voice. If you have, make revisions. Once you have completed writing, re-read your work a final time.

WEEK 2 – Getting Started

THE ESSAY – VOLUME 1 | **LESSON 1**

Student Self-Evaluation

This is your opportunity to **assess your ability to communicate with the active voice**. An honest and thorough evaluation is an opportunity for you to learn from your own writing and move through the process of revision thoughtfully and productively.

Student Name

Assignment   Date

- ❑ Make a thorough sweep of your rough draft, underline all active verbs in red. If you find a passive verb, draw a red box around the verb or verb phrase and change it to an active verb when you revise.

- ❑ Re-read your draft making sure you communicate singularly through the directed sense. Ask yourself if the paragraph precisely describes through the focus of the particular sense.

- ❑ Make a thorough sweep of your paragraph for mechanics—capitalization, punctuation, fragments, run-ons, and tense.

WEEK 2 – Getting Started

BECOME AN ARCHITECT | LESSON 1

SIGHT Paragraph » *Final Draft*
After you have made revisions to your rough draft, copy your work neatly on this page.

WEEK 3 – The Introduction, part 1

THE ESSAY – VOLUME 1 | LESSON 2

Lesson 2: The Introduction, part 1

→ To review, an essay is a short composition of words that communicate a specific idea in a distinct three-part structure (introduction, body, conclusion).

The word *essay* probably originates from the Latin *exagium* meaning "to weigh out" and from the French *essayer* meaning "to try" or "to attempt."

All writing begins with an idea. Inside the structure of an essay the *introduction* is the place where you *introduce* your readers to your idea.

William Wordsworth reminds writers to, "Fill your paper with the breathings of your heart."

Complete this phrase:

An essay is an opportunity for you "_____" an idea
                                    Latin meaning

and "_____" to compose the breathings of your heart.
    French meaning

Define each part of an essay in your own words:

introduction

body

conclusion

WEEK 3 – The Introduction, part 1

BECOME AN ARCHITECT | **LESSON 2**

Now use a dictionary to define:

introduction

idea

➡ The first step in composing an essay is to come up with an idea.

Brainstorming begins with three questions:
1. **What is my idea?**
2. **Why is my idea important?**
3. **Who will be my readers?**

Workbook Assignments »
Complete the following assignments this week in *Thinking in Threes*.
☐ Pages 57–65: "Writing Introductions"
☐ Pages 69-76: "Writing Fluent Sentences"

WEEK 3 – The Introduction, part 1

THE ESSAY - VOLUME 1 | **LESSON 2**

"Voice" Warm-Up »
This warm-up will help you practice different style techniques to develop your voice. Review pages 12—13 and then complete the following exercises.

Place a prepositional phrase in the middle and the end of the sentence:

1. The cat slept for hours *behind* _____, *after* the _____.

Place a clause at the end of the sentence:

2. Josh made an appointment with the dentist because _____.

Insert an appositive:

3. Jordan, _____, was a goalie.

Complete a sentence that begins with an "ing" word:

4. *Sorting* through his notes, _____.

Complete a sentence that begins with an infinitive:

5. *To listen* is _____.

Change the sentences to active voice:

6. The tin can *was crushed* beneath the boy's stomp.

7. The day I forgot my wallet jelly doughnuts *were sold* for a quarter!

Change the sentences to passive voice:

8. I wonder if anyone remembers that Levi Strauss *invented* blue jeans?

9. At the track meet, our team's sprinters *won* at least two races.

WEEK 4 – The Introduction, part 1

BECOME AN ARCHITECT | LESSON 2

Lesson 2: The Introduction, part 1 (cont.)

"Voice" Writing Exercise »

Write Through the Senses: TOUCH

As writers, we gather details that will spark the reader's senses. This week write through the sense of touch, **avoiding all passive verbs**, incorporating, instead, strong, active verbs. Use as many of the voice techniques as possible. Remember, this is a voice exercise and, as such, may sound stilted. **The purpose is to experiment with language to gain the tools that will elevate your voice.**

Example of writing through the sense of *touch*:

> I **leave** my sandals behind and **skip** *barefoot along the dirt path*. Soon I'm **wishing** for the protection of *rubber soles, thorns and sharp rocks* **pricking** my feet *like cactus spines*. I **tip toe** *delicately along the thorny trail*, **squealing** *in pain* every few seconds. The path **rises and gives** way to a valley of granite. Carefully, I **edge** my way *across the slick, steep warm rock slabs. Tiny stones* **roll** *from under my feet* down the slope and into the stream below. After a couple minutes of **hiking** up stream my final destination **comes** into view. Excitement **courses** through me as I discard all caution and **bolt** for my favorite alpine pool. **Piling** my towel and sun hat on a nearby rock, I **peel** off my clothes and head for the water. Before I can **plunge** into the depths of the pool, a sudden thought **hits** me *like a lightning bolt*. Sunscreen! Back at the rock I **squirt** *a blob of white, oily sunscreen into my hand* and begin to **rub** it in. *Brrr! The white goop feels like slimy ice against my warm body*. Now, *sufficiently greasy*, I **steal** to the edge of the small granite cliff and **jump** into the shimmering, turquoise water below. My body **cuts** *the surface cleanly before the mass of chilly liquid* fully **engulfs** me. Shock **slaps** me *across the face. A shutter of shivers* **gushes** through me. *The water's temperature* **numbs** my brain. Reaching the surface, I **welcome** *a huge gulp of air into my lungs*. Frantically, I **splash** *towards the huge rock island* in the center of the deep pool. *Smooth stone* **braces** *underfoot* and I **relax** my breathing, "Wooowee! What cold water!" I **shout** for the wilderness to hear. Desperate for warmth, I **crawl** *up the slick granite slide. The green, slimy algae* **slithers** *under my feet*, making for a treacherous escape from the swimming hole.

Begin your touch paragraph by brainstorming some topic ideas:

_____
_____
_____

Now, generate a list of descriptive sight words:

_____
_____
_____

Finally, compile a list of active verbs you might use for this paragraph:

_____
_____

On the following two pages, write a rough draft and a final draft of your paragraph »

WEEK 4 – The Introduction, part 1

TOUCH Paragraph » *Rough Draft*
Begin drafting your touch paragraph. Use a high lighter to find your verbs and make sure you have not used the passive voice. If you have, make revisions. Once you have completed writing, re-read your work a final time.

WEEK 4 – The Introduction, part 1

BECOME AN ARCHITECT | LESSON 1

Student Self-Evaluation

This is your opportunity to **assess your ability to communicate with the active voice**. An honest and thorough evaluation is an opportunity for you to learn from your own writing and move through the process of revision thoughtfully and productively.

Student Name

Assignment   Date

- ❏ Make a thorough sweep of your rough draft, underline all active verbs in red. If you find a passive verb, draw a red box around the verb or verb phrase and change it to an active verb when you revise.

- ❏ Re-read your draft making sure you communicate singularly through the directed sense. Ask yourself if the paragraph precisely describes through the focus of the particular sense.

- ❏ Make a thorough sweep of your paragraph for mechanics—capitalization, punctuation, fragments, run-ons, and tense.

WEEK 4 – The Introduction, part 1

TOUCH Paragraph » *Final Draft*
After you have made revisions on your rough draft, copy your work neatly on this page.

WEEK 5 – The Introduction, part 2

BECOME AN ARCHITECT | LESSON 3

Lesson 3: The Introduction, part 2

→ The introduction is the first part of the essay's structure. A good introduction will grab the reader's attention with as few as three sentences.

Review the *Structure of an Essay* diagram on page 16.

What is the first sentence of the introduction called?

What is the last sentence of the introduction called?

Review what you have learned in *Thinking in Threes* and create working definitions for:

hook

thesis statement

Use a dictionary to define:

introduction

thesis

WEEK 5 – The Introduction, part 2

THE ESSAY - VOLUME 1 | LESSON 3

The way you craft words and phrases to communicate an original idea within the essay structure is what will make the structure unique. Understanding the elements of good writing will allow you to develop your style as a writer.

Mechanics *"how you structure it"*
The mechanics of writing refers to the use of punctuation, spelling, grammar, and sentence formation, word meaning, agreement, and inflection a writer uses to direct readers through their written work.

Content *"what you say"*
The content of a written work must be carefully crafted to communicate the author's idea in a precise manner within a clear structure. Using vocabulary that is at once vivid and specific helps to set the mood of a piece. Varying the rhythm of sentences suggests tone and attitude.

Voice *"how you say it"*
The writer's voice shapes and controls language for the single purpose of impacting readers.

Don't forget, if you are reading it, someone wrote it. Always remember to think like a reader when you write. The voice of the writer embellishes and breathes life into the structure of an essay.

In your opinion, what makes something good and interesting to read?

_____
_____
_____
_____

List three things you have recently enjoyed reading (book, article, website, blog, etc.) What do you think made it "readable"?

_____
_____
_____
_____
_____

Workbook Assignments »
Complete the following assignments this week in *Thinking in Threes*.
☐ Pages 23-28: "Writing a Thesis"

WEEK 5 – The Introduction, part 2

BECOME AN ARCHITECT | LESSON 3

"Voice" Warm-Up »

This warm-up will help you practice different style techniques to develop your voice. Review pages 12—13 and then complete the following exercises.

Place a prepositional phrase at the beginning and end of the sentence:

1. *With* _____, little Georgie sang the Star Spangled Banner *before* _____.

Place a clause at the beginning and end of the sentence:

2. *Because* _____, the baby cried until the car came to a stop *when* _____.

Insert an appositive at the end of the sentence:

3. The rainbow delighted the small child, _____.

End the sentence with an "ing" word:

4. The English exam was complete so the boy left the classroom _____.

End the sentence with an infinitive:

5. Being a friend means learning to _____.

Change the sentences to active voice:

6. The letter *was mailed* by Sara on her way to the market.

7. The boat *will be sailed* by Amanda this coming weekend at the lake.

Change the sentences to passive voice:

8. My history teacher *reads* Greek Mythology for fun.

9. Our family *uses* the computer so often that I imagine it needs a nap.

WEEK 6 – The Introduction, part 2

Lesson 3: The Introduction, part 2 (cont.)

"Voice" Writing Exercise »

Write Through the Senses: TASTE

As writers, we gather details that will spark the reader's senses. This week write a paragraph through the sense of taste, **avoiding all passive verbs**, incorporating instead strong, active verbs. Use as many of the voice techniques as possible. Remember, this is a voice exercise and, as such, may sound stilted. **The purpose is to experiment with language and gain confidence using the tools that will elevate your voice.**

Example of writing through the sense of *taste*:

> Before too long I **caught** sight of a stand laden with irresistible cotton candy. My *sweet tooth* **begged** me to **whip** out my wallet and **hand** over a ridiculous amount of cash for the classic splurge. **Pushing** the nutrition facts to far corners of my brain, I quickly became the proud owner of a *pink cloud of pure sugar*. With cotton candy in hand, I **pinched** off *a sizable clump* and **placed** *the pink fuzz delicately onto my tongue*. Immediately *my mouth* **sensed** *something special*—not an ordinary dessert. First *a sweet cotton ball of bliss* **enveloped** me, **caressing** *my taste buds*. It felt like a sugary spider web **descending** *on my tongue*. Not two seconds later *the wispy pink cloud* **vanished** and **turned** *into hot pink sugar crystals* that **clustered** together and **coated** *my tongue*. Tauntingly the sweet candy dream **dissolved** and **forced** me to tear another large portion off my mini cotton candy tree. *The texture* **reminded** *me of cotton quilt batting*. I **chuckled** to myself at the thought of trying to **wash** a cotton candy filled quilt. Experimenting, *I attempted to* **lick** *the cotton candy without actually eating it. It turned to magenta granules that* **tickled** *my tongue*.

Begin your taste paragraph by brainstorming some topic ideas:

_____
_____

Now, generate a list of descriptive sight words:

_____
_____

Finally, compile a list of active verbs you might use for this paragraph:

_____
_____

On the following two pages, write a rough draft and a final draft of your paragraph »

WEEK 6 – The Introduction, part 2

TASTE Paragraph » *Rough Draft*

Begin drafting your taste paragraph. Use a highlighter to find your verbs and make sure you have not used the passive voice. If you have, make revisions. Once you have completed writing, re-read your work a final time.

WEEK 6 – The Introduction, part 2

THE ESSAY – VOLUME 1 | LESSON 3

Student Self-Evaluation

This is your opportunity to **assess your ability to communicate with the active voice**. An honest and thorough evaluation is an opportunity for you to learn from your own writing and move through the process of revision thoughtfully and productively.

Student Name

Assignment   Date

- ❑ Make a thorough sweep of your rough draft, underline all active verbs in red. If you find a passive verb, draw a red box around the verb or verb phrase and change it to an active verb when you revise.

- ❑ Re-read your draft making sure you communicate singularly through the directed sense. Ask yourself if the paragraph precisely describes through the focus of the particular sense.

- ❑ Make a thorough sweep of your paragraph for mechanics—capitalization, punctuation, fragments, run-ons, and tense.

WEEK 8 – The Body

BECOME AN ARCHITECT | **LESSON 4**

Student Self-Evaluation

This is your opportunity to **assess your ability to communicate with the active voice**. An honest and thorough evaluation is an opportunity for you to learn from your own writing and move through the process of revision thoughtfully and productively.

Student Name

Assignment   Date

❏ Make a thorough sweep of your rough draft, underline all active verbs in red. If you find a passive verb, draw a red box around the verb or verb phrase and change it to an active verb when you revise.

❏ Re-read your draft making sure you communicate singularly through the directed sense. Ask yourself if the paragraph precisely describes through the focus of the particular sense.

❏ Make a thorough sweep of your paragraph for mechanics—capitalization, punctuation, fragments, run-ons, and tense.

WEEK 8 – The Body

SMELL Paragraph » *Final Draft*

After you have made revisions on your rough draft, copy your work neatly on this page.

WEEK 10 – The Conclusion

BECOME AN ARCHITECT | LESSON 5

Lesson 5: The Conclusion (cont.)

"Voice" Writing Exercise »

Write Through the Senses: HEARING

As writers, we gather details that will spark the reader's senses. This week write a paragraph through the sense of hearing, **avoiding all passive verbs**, incorporating instead strong, active verbs. Use as many of the voice techniques as possible. Remember, this is a voice exercise and, as such, may sound stilted. **The purpose is to experiment with language and gain confidence using the tools that will elevate your voice.**

Example of writing through the sense of *hearing*:

I **walk** slowly through a dim tunnel of eucalyptus trees. Peeling *branches* **groaning** *eerily in wind* form a tangled arch overhead, blocking out all sunlight—*a rickety old rocking chair* **creaking** *back and forth.* *They* **whisper** *to one another in hushed tones.* Leaves **shudder** *like wind chimes.* Still, *rustling* **soothes** me as I **sway** steadily along the branch-strewn path. *My feet* **pad** *softly* upon the forest floor. *Silent thoughts and the pattering steps* **accompany** me on a dream like journey. My imagination **projects** onto my surroundings, a mystical battle scene **unfolds**. My footsteps **transform** into *a plodding horse, hooves* **pounding** *the ground dully. The horse's bit* **clicks** *against its porcelain teeth.* A twig **snaps** *angrily*, and archers **appear** from behind trees. *Grinding metal* **meets** *my ears* as I **unsheathe** *a glinting sword. Whooosh! Arrows* **fly** *through the air and* **twang** *against tree trunks.* Shouts **penetrate** *the eerie calm. Figures* **collide**, *their armor thudding loudly.*
A rustling of leaves **flings** *me from the fray of battle back into reality.*

Begin your hearing paragraph by brainstorming some topic ideas:

_____
_____
_____

Now, generate a list of descriptive sight words:

_____
_____
_____

Finally, compile a list of active verbs you might use for this paragraph:

_____
_____
_____

On the following two pages, write a rough draft and a final draft of your paragraph »

WEEK 10 – The Conclusion

THE ESSAY - VOLUME 1 | **LESSON 5**

HEARING Paragraph » *Rough Draft*
Begin drafting your hearing paragraph. Use a highlighter to find your verbs and make sure you have not used the passive voice. If you have, make revisions. Once you have completed writing, re-read your work a final time.

WEEK 10 – The Conclusion

BECOME AN ARCHITECT | **LESSON 5**

Student Self-Evaluation

This is your opportunity to **assess your ability to communicate with the active voice**. An honest and thorough evaluation is an opportunity for you to learn from your own writing and move through the process of revision thoughtfully and productively.

Student Name

Assignment   Date

- ❏ Make a thorough sweep of your rough draft, underline all active verbs in red. If you find a passive verb, draw a red box around the verb or verb phrase and change it to an active verb when you revise.

- ❏ Re-read your draft making sure you communicate singularly through the directed sense. Ask yourself if the paragraph precisely describes through the focus of the particular sense.

- ❏ Make a thorough sweep of your paragraph for mechanics—capitalization, punctuation, fragments, run-ons, and tense.

WEEK 10 – The Conclusion

THE ESSAY – VOLUME 1 | **LESSON 5**

HEARING Paragraph » *Final Draft*
After you have made revisions to your rough draft, copy your work neatly on this page.

Notes

Notes

Notes

Notes